ARCTURUS

This edition published in 2018 by Arcturus Publishing Limited
26/27 Bickels Yard, 151–153 Bermondsey Street,
London SE1 3HA

Illustrated by: James Lancett
Written by: William Potter
Designed by: Well Nice
Edited by: Sebastian Rydberg

ISBN: 978-1-78828-601-5
CH006204NT
Supplier 29, Date 0818, Print run 6860

Printed in China

PICK YOUR POWER

Check out these heroes' superpowers!
Which awesome abilities would you have?

Fill in the power buttons to activate your hidden abilities!

Superstrength

Flight

Superspeed

Superstink

Stretching

Power blasts

Flame power

Ice power

Walking up walls

Sticky tongue

Superhearing

Turning invisible

X-ray vision

Jumping really high

Remembering long numbers

Supernice

DRAW A HERO

Follow the steps to draw a superstrong hero.

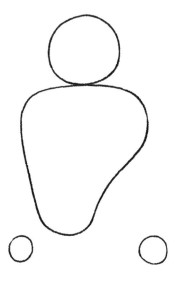

1 Lightly pencil an upturned pear-shaped figure for the torso, circles for the head and hands, plus pointed feet.

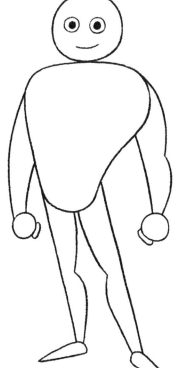

2 Connect the hands and feet to the body. Add a pair of eyes and a mouth.

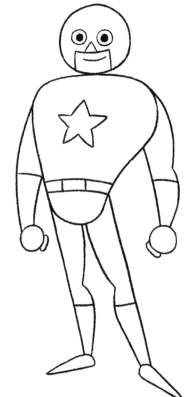

3 Begin adding costume details over the hero's body.

4 You can give your superhero a fancy mask and a cape, too.

Follow the guidelines to draw your first superhero.

DRAW A HEROINE

Follow the steps to draw a superpowered heroine.

1

Lightly pencil a torso and skirt, plus circles for the head and hands.

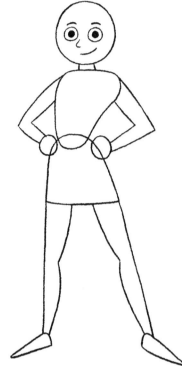

2

Add arms and legs, plus eyes, nose, and a mouth.

3

Begin adding costume details.

4

Give your heroine long, flowing hair and a cape.

Follow the guidelines to draw your own fabulous superheroine.

GET AHEAD!

Time for a close-up! Here's how to draw some heroic heads.

Give your heroes cool masks, glasses, or helmets, too.

TEAM PICK

Stellar Girl is choosing her superteam. Draw the faces of heroes you think should join her squad on the computer screen.

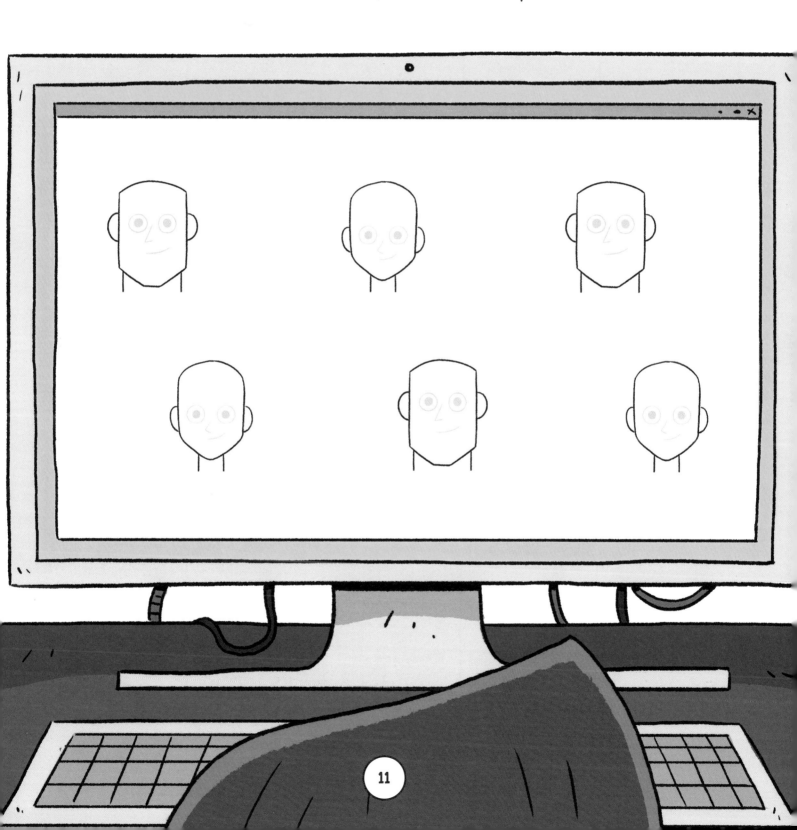

COSTUME PICKER

Roll a dice to decide what the hero on the next page should wear.

	HEADWEAR	BOOTS	EXTRAS	LOGO
1				
2				
3				
4				
5				
6				

Draw the costume and logo designs on the superhero,
following the dice rolls on the last page.

LEAPING INTO ACTION

Get your heroes moving! Here's how to draw jumping champions.

Draw a heroine leaping between these skyscrapers.

SUPERSPEED

Here's how to be fast on the draw with a superspeeding hero.

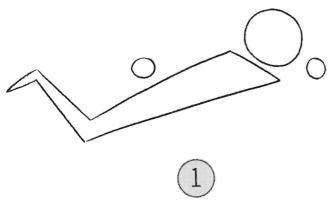

1

The racing superhero is stretched out and leaning forward.

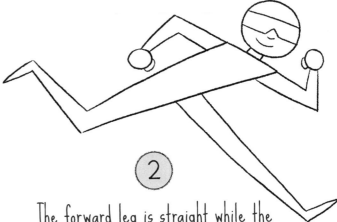

2

The forward leg is straight while the other leg and arms are bent.

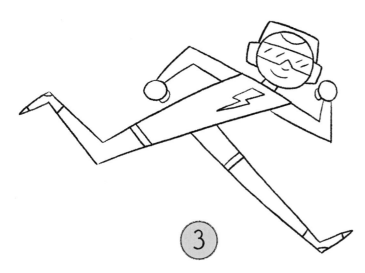

3

Give your speedster a jazzy costume.

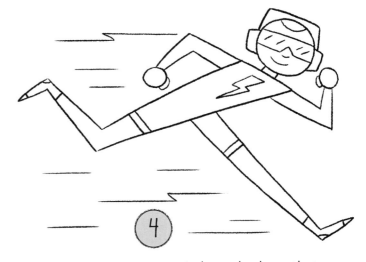

4

Add some speed lines behind the hero that show the direction he's running from.

Draw a hero running to overtake this fast train.
Add speed lines behind him to help him catch up.

HEAVY LIFTING

See these superstrong heroes showing off their muscle power. Some are stronger than others!

What is this hero lifting? Draw a huge weight on his shoulders.
It could be a car, a building, a gorilla—whatever you like!

POWER PUNCHES

Get ready to knock out some bad guys by throwing a punch!

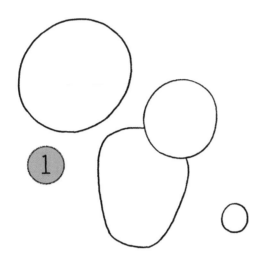

Draw a large circle for a fist and a smaller circle for the head.

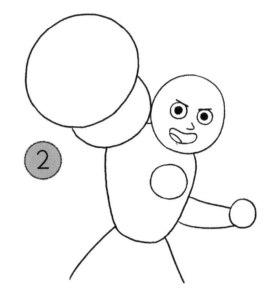

As she punches toward you, her fist looks as big as her head, which is farther back.

Add fingers and a thumb to both hands, plus costume details.

This dynamic figure needs some hair, too.

Draw a heroine punching through a wall.

IN THE SWING

The heroine twists her body as she hurls her power hammer, putting her whole strength into the throw. Action lines show how her body spins and the direction her hammer has been thrown in.

Some heroes carry weapons for throwing. Some pick up whatever's handy to fling at bad guys. What will you choose?

Draw something for this hero to throw.

POWER PLAY

Here are some cool superpowers for you to copy. Add your own below!

Meet the Opposite. His powers cancel out those of his foes.
The right side of his costume is the opposite of the left, with black
instead of white and white instead of black. Finish drawing it for him.

BLAST AWAY

Power blasts can have different effects, making objects disintegrate, knocking villains backward, or even causing explosions.
Here are some ideas for how to draw bombastic bursts.

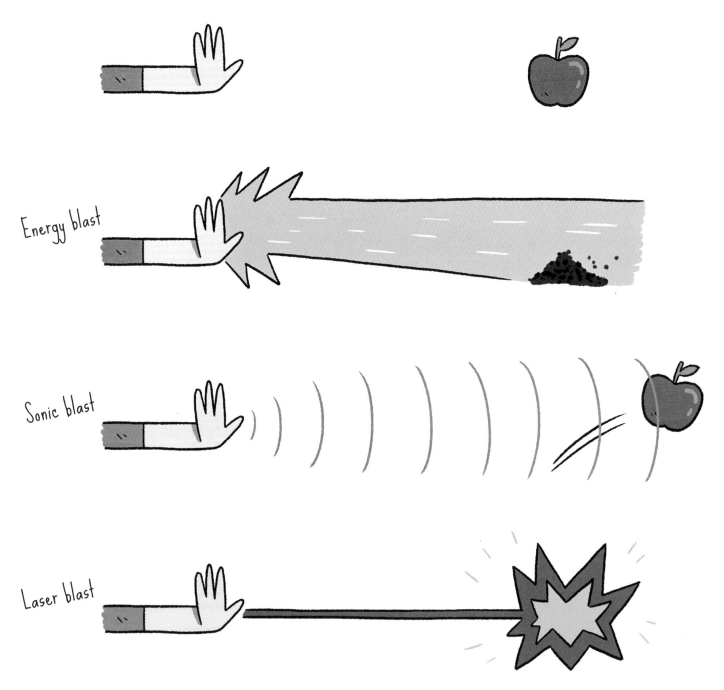

Energy blast

Sonic blast

Laser blast

Help Blast Girl beat the robots by drawing a different blast shooting from each hand and foot!

FULL STRETCH

Being super stretchy is really handy!
Here are some of the things a flexible body can do.
Add your own ideas below!

REACH HIGH INTO THE SKY

SQUEEZE UNDER A DOOR

CROSS THE ROAD-OVER THE TRAFFIC!

FIT INTO A TIGHT SPOT

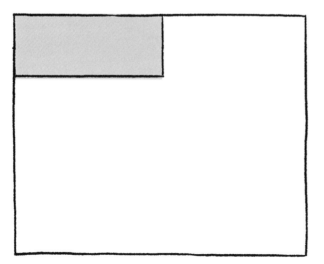

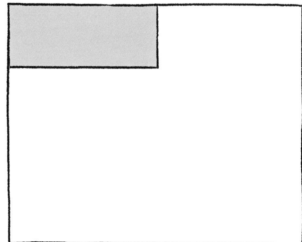

Attach the hero's body to his head, hands, and feet
by drawing his arms and legs stretching around the obstacles.

SUPER SENSES

Give your heroes some sensory superpowers!
See, listen, touch, smell. What else can your hero do?

What crime has the heroine seen with her X-ray vision?
Draw the view through the wall.

BANK

MEET THE NASTIES

Bring on the bad guys, the worst of the worst. They have an evil look in their eyes that tells you they are planning something wicked.

Villains often choose greens and purples for their scary suits. They get them from a secret supervillain clothes store.

This villain is striking a menacing pose.

Draw your own bad guy over this outline,
with a wicked-looking machine in his hands.

BULKING UP

Follow the steps to draw a big and bulky supervillain.

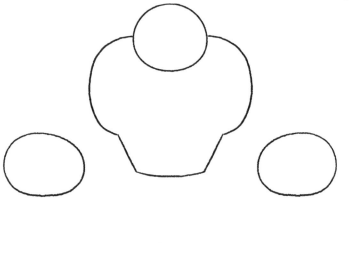

1 Draw three circles for the head and fists, plus a wide upper body.

2 Add muscled arms and legs, plus a mean face.

3 Add zigzag lines where huge muscles have ripped his costume.

4 Draw a few crosses and scuff marks to show that he's been in a fight.

When this puny evildoer presses a button on his belt, he bulks up into a muscled menace. Draw the musclebound bully he becomes.

FIRE GUY

This hero can turn to flames and fire superhot blasts.
Here's how to draw a flaming superstar.

Use rows of curvy zigzags to show flames.
Add a few red leaf shapes for stray flames.

Add flames around the fiery hero and a jet of flame as he barbecues a massive marshmallow for a giant hero.
Add some dark patches on the marshmallow as it cooks.

COLD AS ICE

Follow the steps to bring a frosty fiend to life!

1

2

3

4

For ice blasts, draw a straight line with jagged icicles hanging underneath.

For a frosty ice block, draw a rough shape with angled sides and a few lines to show dark reflections in the ice. Add a puddle of melted ice below it.

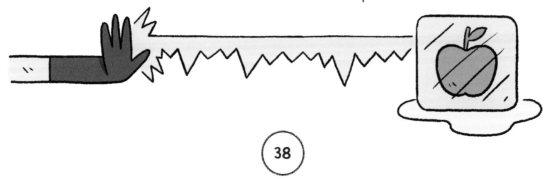

Ms. Winter is too cool for the hero to deal with. Draw her ice blast hitting the hero and a frosty ice block over him.
Add icicles and snow to the background ... and maybe a snowman.

TOUGH STUFF

Some superheroes and villains can change their bodies into wood, metal, and rock. Here's how to draw supertough skin.

SKIN

WOOD

Draw wood with wrinkly lines that look like rough bark. Add a few sprouting twigs and leaves.

METAL

A metal finish is smooth and shiny. Leave some white diagonal lines to show reflections.

STONE

Stone has a jagged outline with cracks, dashes, and spots that show a rough texture.

Draw the different finishes on the skin of these supervillains.

THE BOULDER!

He needs to get rocky and has a few pebbles falling off him.

BARK BOY!

He needs a wooden finish, with added twigs and leaves.

SALLY STEEL!

She can change her skin to—you guessed it—steel! Give her body a shiny metal finish.

SUPERSIZED

Mountain Man can grow to the size of, well, a mountain!
His pal, Flea Girl, can shrink to the size of an insect,
and ride a jumping flea like a horse.

To show how big or small your heroes are,
you just need to draw something next to
them to see the scale.

Copy the hero one square at a time, from the small grid to a large one, to show him as a giant.

STORMS AHEAD

Lightning Conductor is using her weather wand to bring down bolts of lightning. Follow the steps to bring on the bad weather!

Draw a loop in a line of curly curves for the bottom edge of a storm cloud. You can add parallel lines of rain, too.

To make a lightning bolt, draw two big, bold zigzags that join at the tip.

Add storm clouds and rain to this scene, plus lightning bolts coming from Lightning Conductor's wand.

INTO BATTLE

What happens when superheroes and villains meet?
Do they sit down for a chat and cup of tea? No!
They fight!

These are some action poses—showing battling heroes and villains—for you to copy.

Fire eye blasts and flame balls between the fighting superteams.
Add some explosions, too!

MAKE SOME NOISE!

Are your action scenes too quiet? Time to add some sound effects!

Make the sound of a punch, a blast, or an explosion with your mouth. Now, try to spell it. The wilder the spelling, the better.

Use rough and ragged, chunky letters to write your sound effects on the page, with the word coming from the source of the sound.

Add your own noises to this explosive battle, following the dotted lines.

NOW YOU'RE TALKING

Get your superheroes chatting to each other with speech bubbles.

Here are different types you can use.

Add your own words in speech bubbles to this comic book scene,
plus a sound effect for the final punch!

FIND THE FACE

Roll a dice to choose facial expressions for the heroes and villains on the next page.

1 = HEROIC

2 = EVIL

3 = WORRIED

4 = LAUGHING

5 = ANGRY

6 = SLEEPY

Give each of these heroes and villains the
expression decided by the roll of the dice.

DRAW YOUR WEAPONS

Not all heroes and villains have superpowers. Some use fighting skills and high-tech weapons to tackle their foes.

Here are some fancy devices you can hand out to your characters.

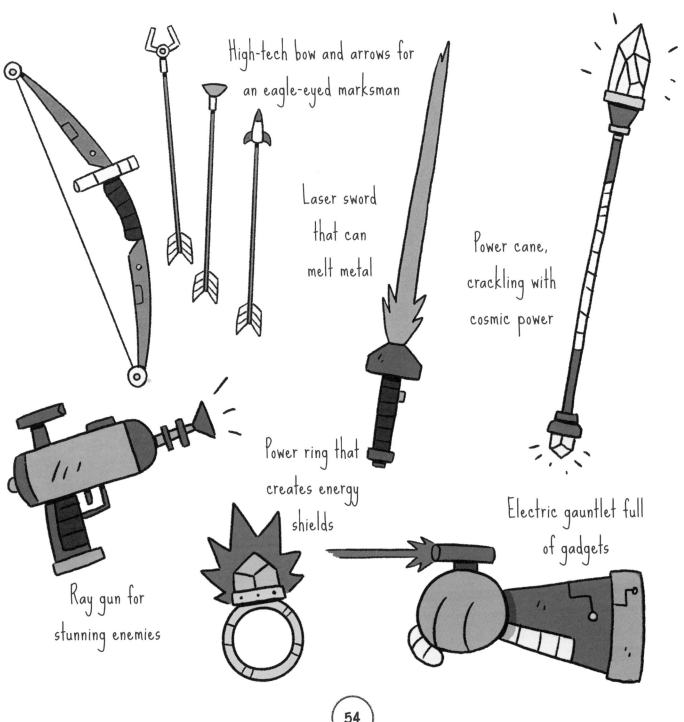

High-tech bow and arrows for an eagle-eyed marksman

Laser sword that can melt metal

Power cane, crackling with cosmic power

Power ring that creates energy shields

Ray gun for stunning enemies

Electric gauntlet full of gadgets

Draw weapons—staffs, bows and arrows, and blasters—in the hands of the heroes and villains.

WILD RIDE

If your hero can't fly or run at superspeed,
they'll need a cool vehicle to drive.
Give it some crazy crime-fighting gadgets, too!

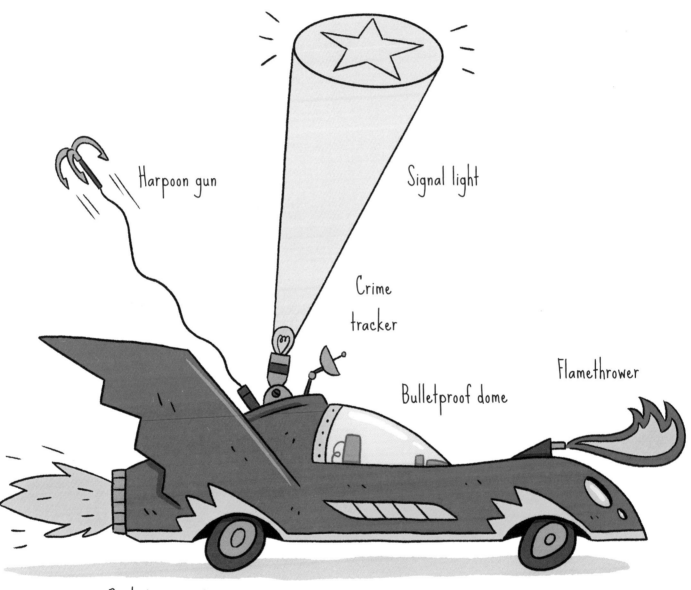

Harpoon gun

Signal light

Crime
tracker

Bulletproof dome

Flamethrower

Rocket-powered engine

Ejector seat

Draw an amazing vehicle for this superheroine to race in.

SECRET IDENTITY

Do your heroes have a secret life when they are not fighting crime?
Are some of these people secretly superheroes or villains?

THE MILLIONAIRE

THE HOTSHOT REPORTER

THE GEEKY STUDENT

THE TOP SCIENTIST

Draw a disguise over these heroes' costumes.
You could add casual clothes, a uniform, hat, glasses, or a fake beard!

HERO HQ

Heroes hang out at secret headquarters.
Here are some super-places for super-bases.

The mountaintop hideout

Underwater base

Top-secret cave

Skyscraper HQ

Look at what you can expect to find at their base.

Launchpad

Science lab

Crime-detecting computer

Trophies

Meeting room

Coffee machine and mugs

Fill this secret underground base with everything your superheroes need.

ANIMAL ANTICS

Some heroes and villains have powers based on animals.
Roll a dice to decide which animal features to give to the superheroes
and villains on the next page.

1 = FANGS

2 = SPIKES

3 = EARS

4 = SHARK FIN

5 = BUG EYES

6 = TRUNK

Add animal features to the heroes and villains
on this page as decided by the dice.

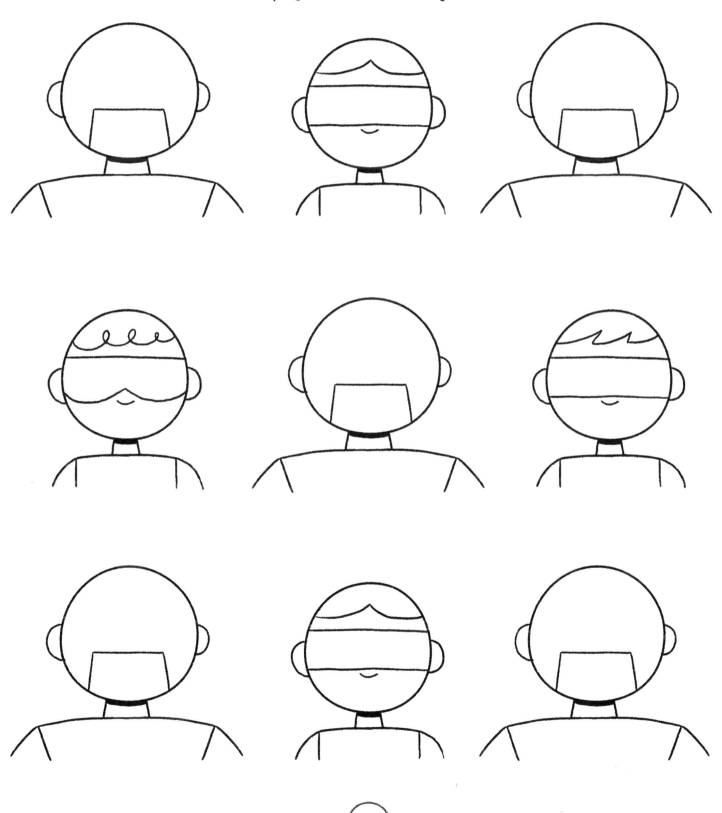

MACHINE MENACE

Follow the steps to turn this supervillain into a sinister cyborg.

Here is the standard supervillain in a dramatic pose.

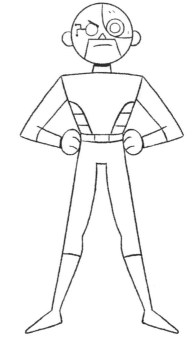

One eye is replaced by a camera lens.

Replace the arms and legs with stronger metal limbs.

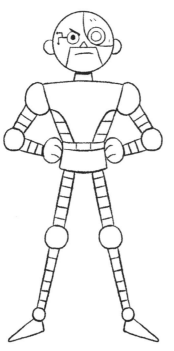

Add electronic ears with aerials and a nuclear power cell on the chest.

Not all cyborgs are villains! This one is a superheroine.
Draw the right-hand side of her body with robot parts.

POWER SUIT

A super scientist has designed her own hi-tech suit to become a soaring superhero. Here are the clever parts she has invented.

Helmet with internal computer readouts

Lightweight, blast-proof metal plating

Power gloves with finger blasters

Jet boots

Now the scientist is giving her invention a test drive.
Finish drawing Rocket Woman's suit! Did she give it a coat of paint?

UNDERSEA SUPERHERO

Follow the steps to draw a swimming superhero.

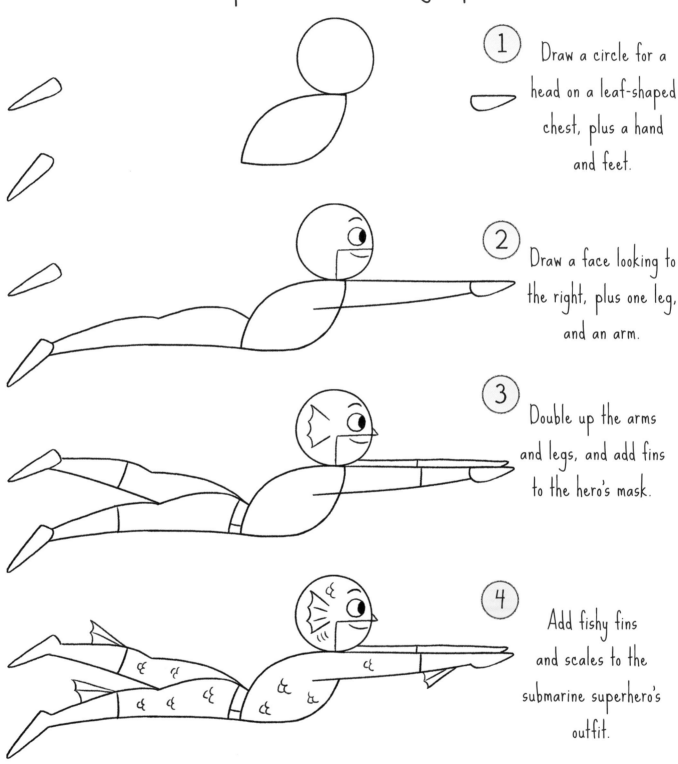

1 Draw a circle for a head on a leaf-shaped chest, plus a hand and feet.

2 Draw a face looking to the right, plus one leg, and an arm.

3 Double up the arms and legs, and add fins to the hero's mask.

4 Add fishy fins and scales to the submarine superhero's outfit.

Copy the ocean hero into an underwater world, with fish, seaweed, corals, and sunken ruins. Who or what is racing him?

RADIOACTIVE ROGUE

Follow the steps to draw a dripping, radioactive supervillain.

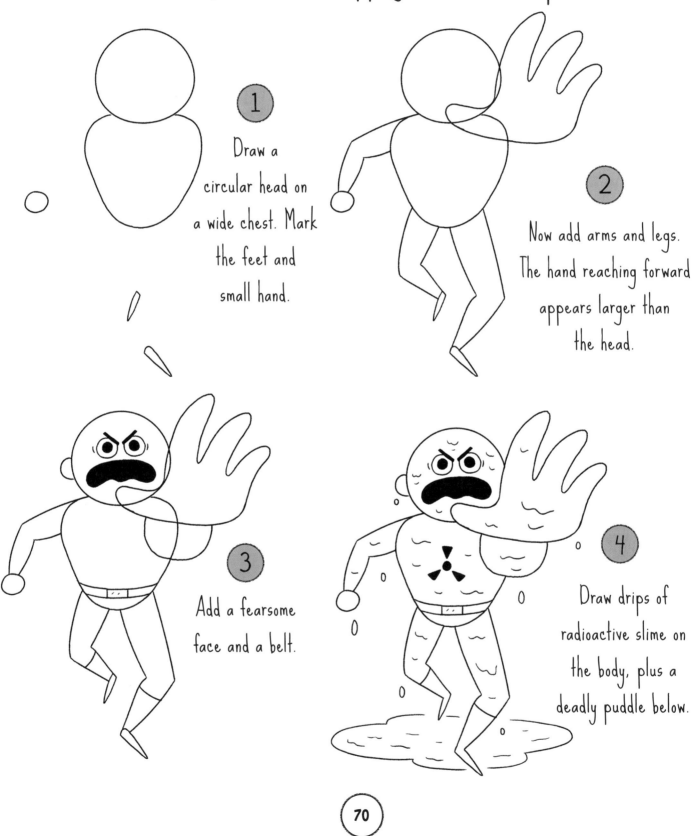

1 Draw a circular head on a wide chest. Mark the feet and small hand.

2 Now add arms and legs. The hand reaching forward appears larger than the head.

3 Add a fearsome face and a belt.

4 Draw drips of radioactive slime on the body, plus a deadly puddle below.

Add drips, blobs, and puddles to this molten monster.
Include some footprints melted into the ground behind him.

GALACTIC GREATS

Take your heroes to space! Here's a cast of characters to get you started.

Human astronauts defend our planet from alien invasion. They use jetpacks when they leave their starships.

A galactic police force brings order to distant worlds. This alien has a power belt to protect him in deep space.

This space heroine explores the universe using cosmic powers. Her powers let her travel at light speed and fire cosmic blasts.

Add your own galactic heroes to this page. Are they fighting an alien invader? Complete the space background with stars and planets.

STAR LEECH

Space is full of weird stuff. Try drawing this alien mutant monster.

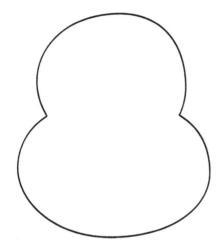

1 Lightly draw a large, curvy blob.

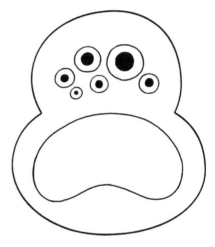

2 Draw lots of eyes in different sizes above a wide-open mouth.

3 Add sharp teeth, spikes, and several curvy tentacles.

4 Draw bumps on the body and a wriggly tongue.

Turn these shapes into alien invaders and strange space creatures.

SUPER SIDEKICKS

Not all heroes work alone. Some train young sidekicks
to help them take on criminals.

1 Sidekicks can
have attitude.

2 Sidekicks are
often acrobats with
martial arts skills.

3 You can give your sidekick
a similar costume to their
grown-up partner.

Design sidekicks for these adult heroes.
Their costumes can match the grown-up versions.

HISTORICAL HEROES

Take some tips from the history books
for these classic heroes.

1

Look at pictures of Greek and
Roman gods and warriors for
costume and weapons ideas.

2

Ancient gods were like superheroes,
with huge strength and powers over
the weather and animals.

3

Why not try a more recent
warrior, like a swashbuckler
from the seven seas?

Turn this hero into a Viking warrior with a helmet, hammer, belt, and beard.

Turn this superheroine into a Roman goddess with a spear, shield, and sandals.

POWER PETS

Your heroes might have pets, too—pets with superpowers! Here are some ideas for animals with amazing talents.

Give this cat and dog superpowers and costumes.
Then, fill their bowls with "superfood."

WHEN GOOD TURNS BAD

Uh-oh! This superhero's turned superbad! Here's how you can tell.

Look at his face, scowling and twisted! Eek! His expression is mean and frowning.

The dark version of the hero has a matching costume in darker shades. And his cape is ragged.

The evil version has a more menacing pose.

Draw a dark version of this happy heroine.

DANGER! DANGER!

Heroes have weaknesses as well as strengths.
What could foil your brave champions?

What is this villain holding that is putting the hero in pain?

LOCK UP

What do you do with a bad guy once you've captured him? You need a superstrong prison. Copy the supervillain square by square behind the bars of the power-proof cage on the next page.

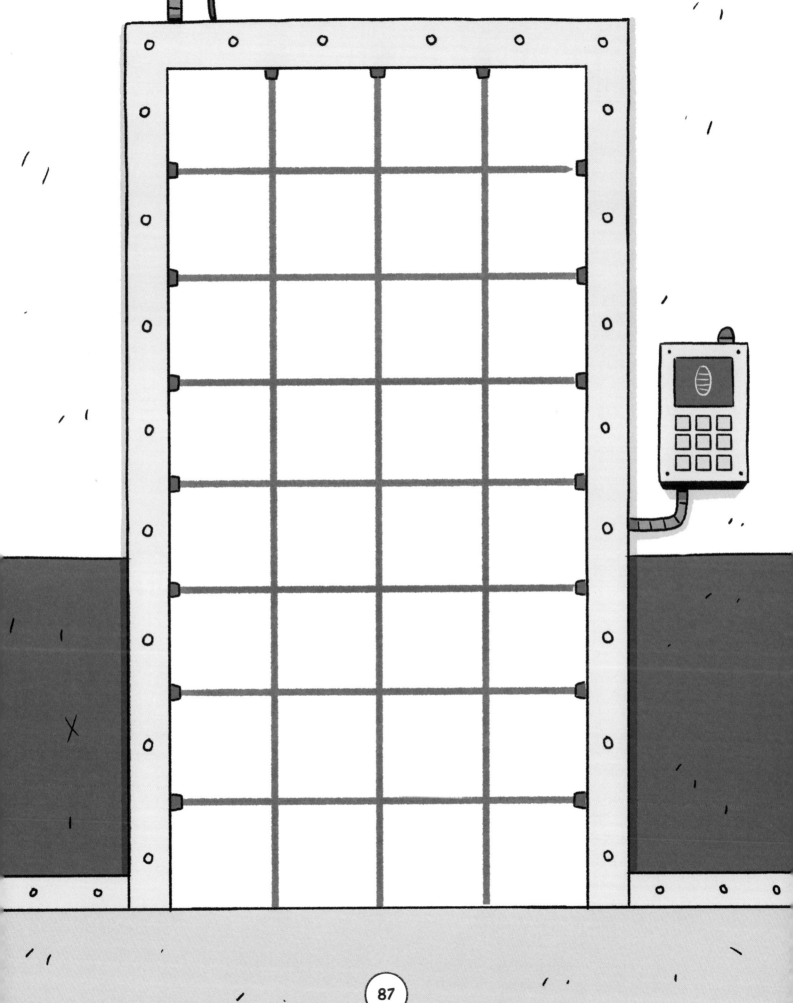

GREAT GADGETS

Some heroes use cool gadgets to fight villains.
Power up your superstars with these devices.

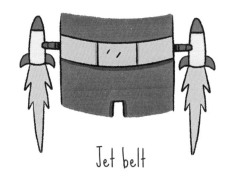

Force ring that can fire many
different blasts

Magical amulet
that can reach into
other dimensions

Jet belt

Power crystal that makes
thoughts become real

Force glove that creates cold,
heat, and force fields

This hero is ready for anything, since she has collected gadgets from all her previous adventures. Draw some crime-busting tools around her neck, in her hand, and on her utility belt.

JET AWAY

International champions need to get around the world fast.
Design a superjet for a superhero.

Make your jet aerodynamic with a
flaming rocket engine.

Add some energy blasts
on the wings.

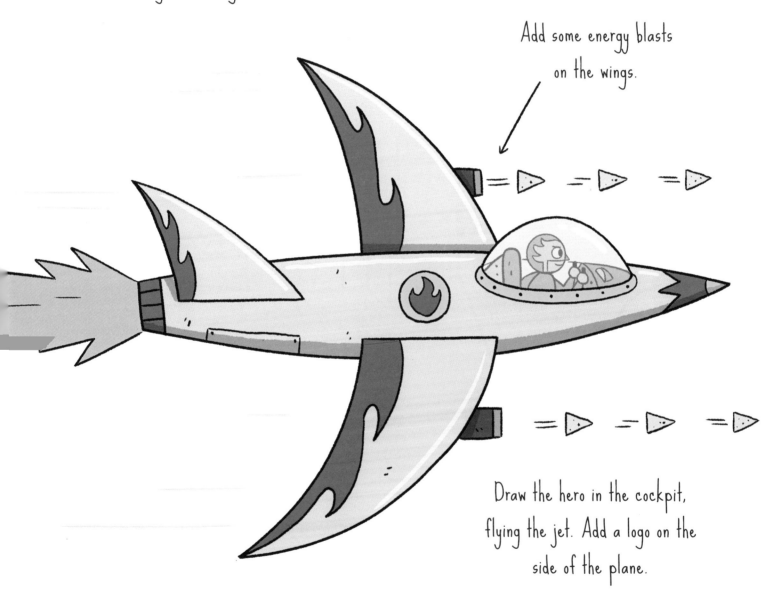

Draw the hero in the cockpit,
flying the jet. Add a logo on the
side of the plane.

Draw an amazing aircraft around your pilot hero.

SHOWDOWN

A comic book adventure tells the story using panels. Follow the action as the hero, Captain Cosmic, breaks free of Rockette's trap.

Can Captain Cosmic keep Rockette from sending a massive meteor toward Earth? Over to you! Finish the final panel, adding your own words and sound effects.

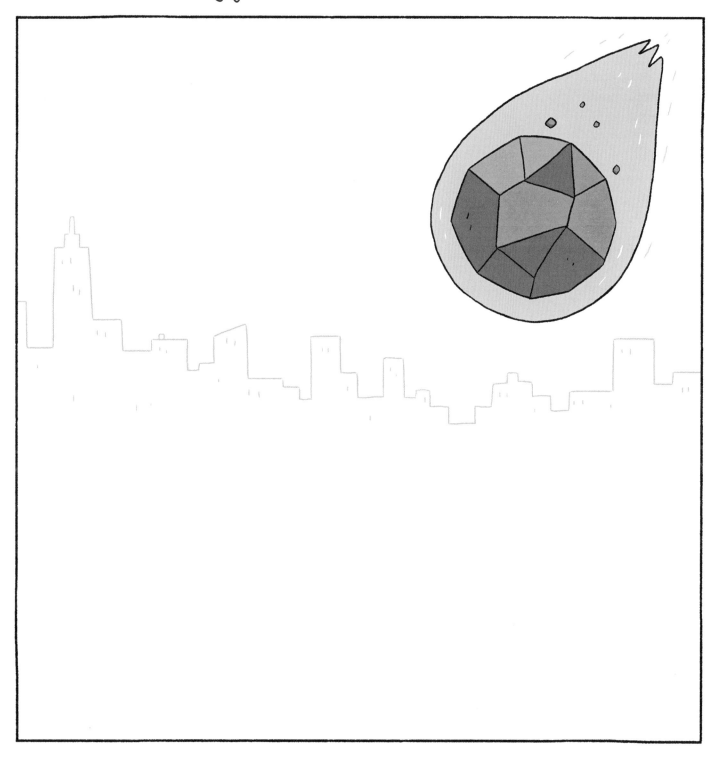

MAGIC MASTER

Anything can happen when magic's involved! Magic powers have changed these heroes in different ways.

Hard luck! This hero's been turned into a statue.

This hero's been made into a monkey!

He's cute as a baby but too tiny to fight crime.

Now, he's ballooned in size!

What magical effect has happened to the heroes? You decide!

RAMPAGING ROBOT

Mighty Maiden has taken apart a dangerous robot!
Look at all the different robot parts. How do they fit together?

Draw another robot for Mighty Maiden to fight. Use the parts from the last page or any other parts you can dream up.

CITYSCAPE

A criminal gang is planning an attack on the city.
Where will they choose to raid first? Here are some places you can include in your superhero's home city.

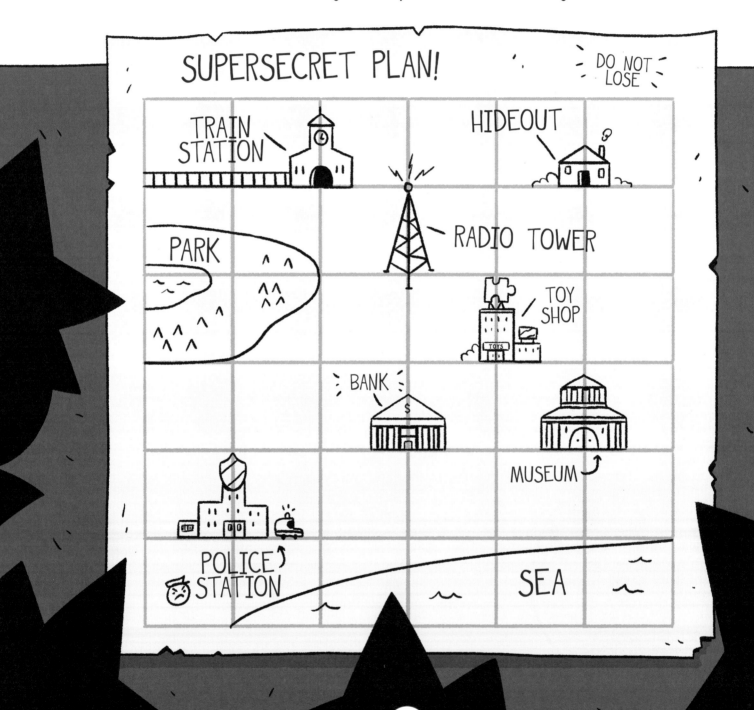

Copy the buildings onto this map. You can choose where to place them, and add some ideas of your own.

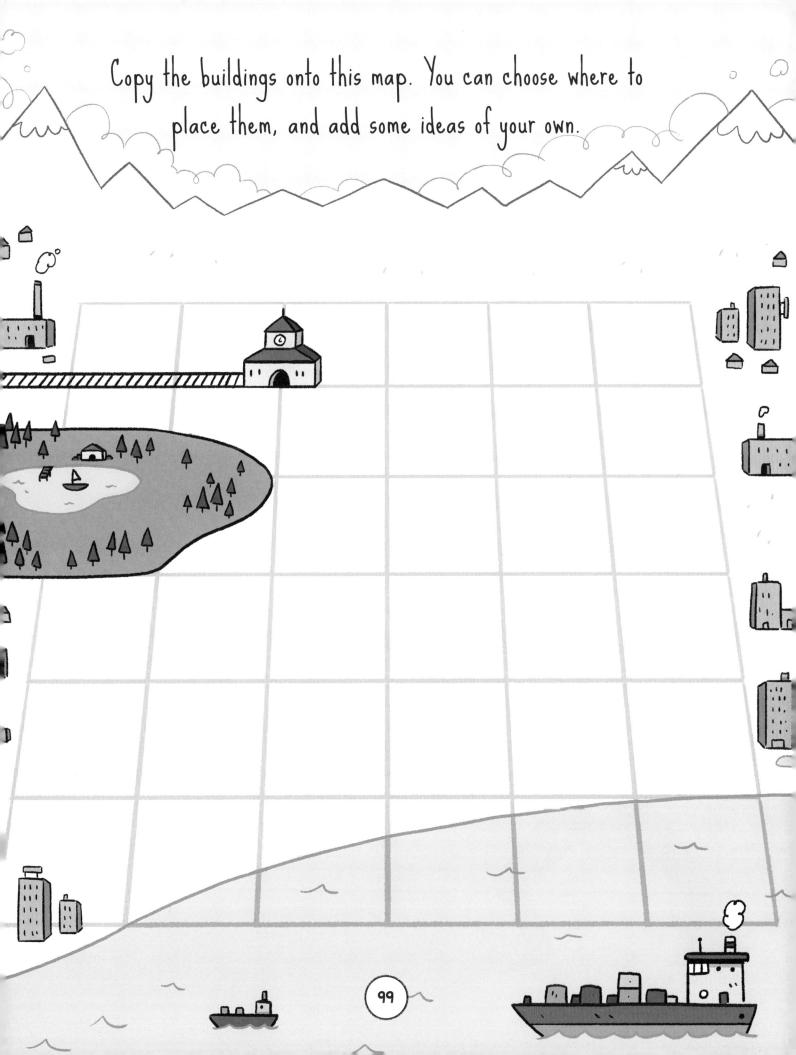

SUPER SAGA

Let's create a cool comic story! Here's a cast of characters to get you started.

(1)   VOLTEEN: This teen hero can zap villains with electrical charges and create blinding light bursts.

(2)

BRAIN DRAIN: This evil scientist plans to make everyone on the planet dumber, so she can rule as Earth's cleverest person.

(3)

THUGBOY: Brain Drain's beefy helper has steel-strong skin and the strength of 10 men.

Use the characters from the last page to complete this comic strip.
You can choose what they say.

FOUL FACES

What a gruesome gallery! You can tell these bad guys have evil plans afoot from their mean expressions.

1 This clever criminal is plotting something dastardly.

2 What made this muscly menace so angry?

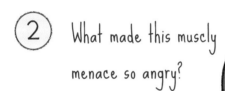

3 When the sinister lady is cackling, you know it's not funny.

These heroes have been shrunk down to toy size. Which evil villain has turned them into playthings for his chessboard? You decide by drawing a villain gloating over the game.

SPINNING AROUND

Action lines show the direction of movement.
These show the swing of a punch, a kick, or a spin.
Try drawing your own hero in action!

Supervillain the Tempest has created a huge tornado to stop the heroes. Draw them battling through the storm, dodging trees, furniture, cars, and other objects.

COSMIC KING

Follow the steps to draw a powerful cosmic being.

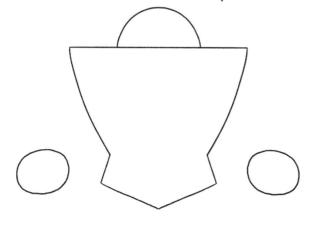

1. Draw a shield-shaped body with a round head and fists.

2. Add bold arms and legs, plus detail on the head.

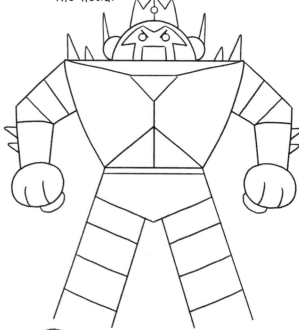

3. Connect shapes on the chest for a robotic look. Add a crest and ears to the head.

4. Give your cosmic being shoulder spikes and lines on his limbs.

A giant cosmic being has arrived on Earth. Is he here to help us or to take over the planet?
Copy the Cosmic King from the last page as he towers over the buildings.

DUPLICATION DANGER

Doctor Diabolical has made things tough for the heroes by using his duplicator. Finish drawing his machine with lots of complicated parts.

Draw lots and lots of evil clones attacking the heroes.

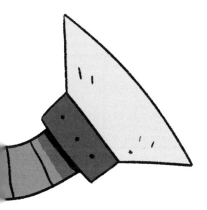
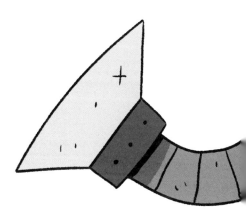

IT'S A TRAP!

Superheroes need to be on the lookout for danger. Supervillains are always laying traps for them. Here are some traps to watch out for.

GRABBING CLAWS

CRUSHING WALLS

NASTY NETS

CHALLENGING CHAINS

HYPNO-RAY

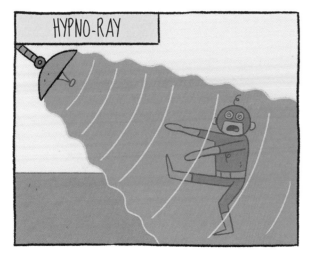

SHARP SPIKES

Design a trap to catch this superhero.

TEAM TOGETHER

Assemble your superteam. Here are the types of heroes you need on your side.

A leader: This needs to be someone the rest of the team will respect. He or she should be good at making battle plans.

Brainy type: You need a hero who can understand and use technology to stop clever supervillains.

Superstrong type: You have to have some muscle to take on the big bad guys.

At least one hero needs to fly, so that they can get places fast and keep teammates from falling from great heights.

Sassy youngster: Being in a superteam should be fun, too. Invite a young joker to work at your side.

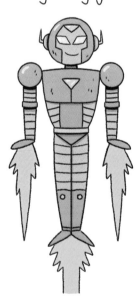

A rich superhero: Someone has to pay the rent on headquarters, as well as repairs on cars and jets!

Which awesome heroes will make the cut?
Draw your assembled superteam.

UNDERWORLD

Superheroes need to be ready for attacks from below ground, too.
There may be secret armies of mole monsters ready to invade the surface.

In the darkness, the cave dwellers need large eyes to see. Their skin is pale from lack of sunlight.

Huge mole monsters live in the deepest caves.

Using underground metals, the cave dwellers have built huge digging machines.

Unused to bright sunlight, the cave dwellers need special glasses to protect their eyes.

The cave dwellers use stun staffs to knock out their enemies.

Giant drills are made ready for a sudden attack on the surface.

The heroes' picnic is about to be disturbed by underground invaders!
Draw the villains preparing to attack.

GROWING MENACE

Imagine a supervillain that can control all plant life.
He has to have a green costume, of course!

The plant controller would use cactus spines as darts.

He would grow flowers that stink!

Vines make perfect ropes for tying up heroes.

Ouch! Watch out for the thorns.

Draw your hero being attacked by everything from the garden!

FAMOUS FAMILY

This superfamily share similar powers, so the parents and kids can go on adventures together!

The mother is the leader, since she's the smartest and fastest and can get everyone out of bed on time.

The dad does all the heavy work. He's superstrong and has a good heart.

The youngest of the team is still getting used to her powers of levitation, but she's as brave as all the rest.

As a teen, the boy with martial arts skills is not sure about hanging out with his parents. Maybe it's time for a solo career.

It's time to create your own fantastic family!
Show them in similar costumes with different powers.
You could give them a power pet, too!

NIGHT RAIDER

This superhero only goes out at night. That's when most criminals are around, too! He wears a dark costume and tries to look scary.

This hero can't fly. He swings between buildings on his own extending cable.

The dark mask gives bad guys a fright. It also hides his secret identity.

The dark cape helps him hide in the shadows.

To back up his combat skills, the hero carries many crime-fighting gadgets in his belt.

Draw lots of triangular pieces of broken glass
as the hero of the night smashes through a window.

FUTURE WORLD

Some heroes travel through time and visit the future. But what will it look like? Here are some ideas.

Clothes keep you warm in any temperature and can check your daily health.

Cars and even trains fly using antigravity engines.

Some towers stretch above the clouds, with elevators entering space.

Most work is done by robots, so humans can study new ideas, be creative, and enjoy free time.

But not everyone is happy. Some villains are using advanced tech to create deadlier weapons. Heroes are still needed!

Our space hero has journeyed to a futuristic world.
Draw what it looks like.

UPGRADE

It's time for an upgrade. This hero's costume and powers are in need of updating. Compare the old and the new versions.

The new costume is made from a modern bulletproof material.

No more laundry! This clever costume cleans itself.

A flameproof layer has been added to the suit.

A built-in computer provides info and keeps the hero in touch with teammates.

Draw a new, fancy modern costume for this hero, too.

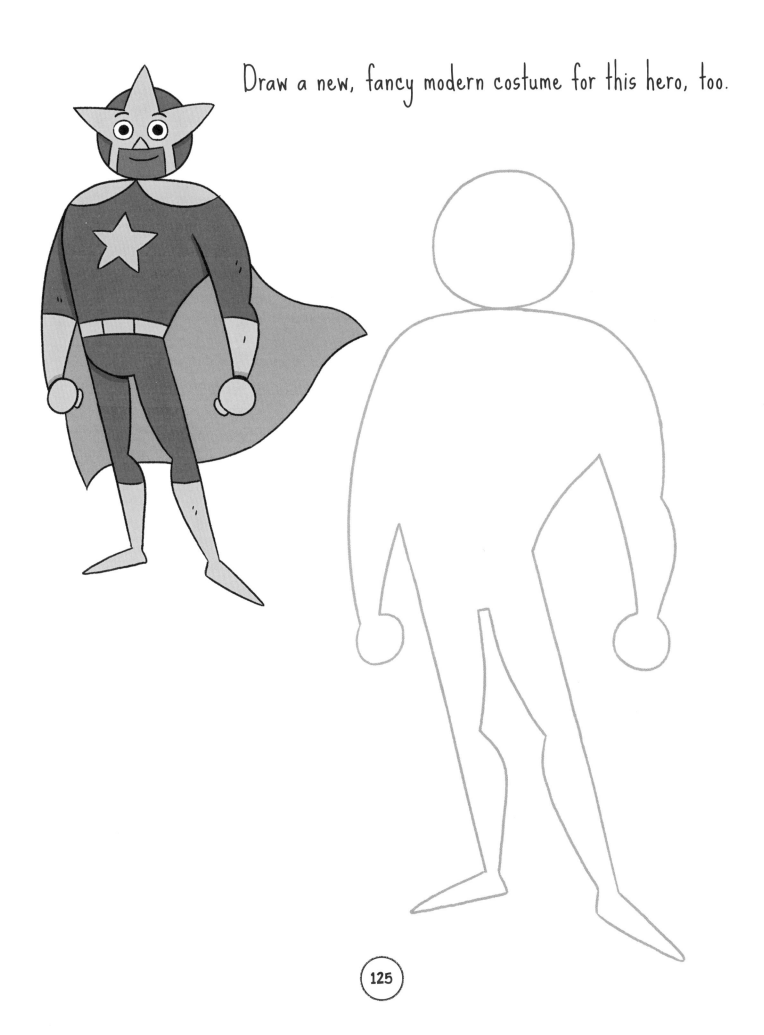

HEADLINE NEWS

Superheroes are in the news again! But not every newspaper likes them!

WIND WOMAN PUTS OUT FIRE

SWIM KING RESCUES WHALE

BUG-MAN— HERO OR MENACE?

Fill in the picture to go with the headline. What do the monster and hero look like?

THE SUPER SCOOP

HERO KEEPS MONSTER FROM EATING THE CITY

Draw a comic book front cover for your own superheroes.
Write the name of the comic in chunky letters across the top.

50 © ISSUE 01 **DRAWING LAB COMICS**